The Fight for the Promiseland

The Fight for the Promiseland

Battle Strategies for Victorious People

Cheryl Cook

Copyright © 2026 Cheryl Cook

For permission requests, please contact the Permissions Coordinator at:

J Merrill Publishing, Inc.
2323 W 5th Avenue, Suite 120
Columbus, OH 43204
www.JMerrill.pub

Paperback ISBN-13: 978-1-961475-63-2
eBook ISBN-13: 978-1-961475-64-9

Book Title: The Fight for the Promiseland
Author: Cheryl Cook

The Expectations
of Promises

I remember being seven years old when my mom promised that my friend Karen could come over on Thursday after we finished our second-grade spelling words to make cookies. The anticipation of baking with my best friend was so thrilling it filled my mind for days.

Looking back as I write this book, I realize that while children have these hopes about promises, so do adults.

Perhaps it begins as a whisper, a thought, a nudge—something we glimpse or daydream about through eyes that see beyond the present.

How often have we spent thousands of dollars on beauty products or exercise equipment because of a promise we saw online or on a shopping channel? We don't know if those things will deliver the results we hope for, yet curiosity propels us forward. We imagine what could be, take small actions, and convince ourselves that this might be the answer.

Have you ever purchased one of those three day body flushes, hoping to lose five pounds before an important event?

The Expectations of Promises

What's compelling about these anticipated promises is how they shape not only our self-perception, but also the way we hope others will see us. Promises can become powerful motivators for both internal and external transformation. Once embraced, a promise can cling to us like honey to the honeycomb—or linger like a haunting movie memory, leaving a pit of anxiety long after the credits roll.

Thoughts emerge from these promises—some spark excitement and curiosity, while others stir hesitation or disbelief. We wonder: Could this really happen for me? That sense of amazement can ignite our spirit, but without guidance, it may fade as quickly as a firework that never reaches its full brilliance.

In the process of change and transformation, especially as women, we often hear messages like, "You can't do that," or "That will never work." Many people face these limiting voices—whether from within or from those around us. Such voices can rob us, like weeds choking out growth and sunlight in a flourishing garden.

Yet even in quiet moments of disappointment, there remains the gentle whisper of God: Try again. Dream again. Hope again. Believe again. It's that inner question rising in our hearts: What if this works? Could I, too, step into God's plans—the good plans, the glorious expected end?

The answer is yes—but it comes at a cost: time, planning, resources, faith, and, above all, trust in the Almighty. It also requires a strategic mindset and an intentional plan. Success demands focus, a willingness to be coached, and a readiness to grow to the next level.

"In all thy ways acknowledge Him, and He shall direct thy paths."

Gideon, before facing battle, sought the Lord for guidance. So we, too, seek Him in our prayers:

Heavenly Father, our rock, our strength, our fortress, and strong deliverer—

We seek You with surrendered hearts, wills, and minds. We believe Your word that no good thing will You withhold from us. We walk in faith and trust that the battle is always won on every front, and we are strong and mighty in You to fight. Amen.

Be strong in the Lord and in the power of His might. We partner with You in words, action, and trust that we can be mighty.

I've witnessed this same struggle in countless women, which is why I wrote this book—to offer guideposts for your own journey to the Promised Land, leading you with clarity, focus, and precision.

Why Do We Have to Fight for What's Promised?

I can already hear the question: Why did the children of Israel have to fight for something that was already promised? Why must we fight for what God has said is ours?

At first, it seems like a paradox. If something has been given, why must we still strive for it? Yet the truth is this: God's promises require our partnership. He may hand us the map, but we must still make the journey. We're called to fight the good fight of faith—not with physical weapons, but with spiritual ones: prayer, perseverance, and obedience.

Throughout this book, we'll follow the story of the children of Israel as they journey toward their Promised Land. Their challenges were not only physical, but also mental and spiritual. They focused on external obstacles and ignored the inner strength God was trying to develop in them—the endurance to continue, the faith to trust, and the courage to possess what was already theirs.

The Promised Land represented more than a destination; it symbolized a better life—for themselves, their children, and generations to come. When things didn't unfold as expected, they lost sight of the promise and had nothing internal to sustain them.

In these pages, we'll explore the internal strategies that could have helped them see beyond the wilderness—and that can help you, too.

This book uses Israel's journey as a historical and spiritual backdrop to reveal what motivates change, what hinders progress, and what we must conquer to claim our own Promised Lands—whether in relationships, finances, purpose, or personal growth.

Your Promised Land is not merely a place—it's a mindset, a belief that something better awaits you and your family. Within these chapters, you'll discover seven principles designed to help you fight wisely, stay focused, and stretch toward the promises God has for you.

Chapter 1
Why Do I Have to Fight?

I've never considered myself a fighter—but I'll admit, I occasionally enjoy watching a good boxing match. There's something fascinating about the moment before the bell rings. Each boxer stands in their corner, lost in an inner world—mentally preparing, sharpening focus, and drawing on every ounce of training to maintain stamina and clarity for what's about to unfold.

Think of the classic Rocky and Creed movies. We get a ringside seat to the fighter's journey—their struggles, discipline, pain, and ultimate determination. We watch them fail, rebuild, and rise again. The fight we see in the ring is only the visible part; the real battle begins long before the lights come on. Tearing down strongholds and arguments that oppose the knowledge of God is where the deepest work happens.

Just like those fighters, we too must "square up" for the battles that shape our future. Whether the fight is for your peace, your purpose, your family, or your promise, it requires an intentional plan. Entering any arena—a game, a mission, a spiritual pursuit without preparation is like starting a journey without a map. Without clarity about where you're headed or how you'll begin, you can end up anywhere. A pilot, before taking off, must establish clarity in the air and anticipate possible weather. Adjustments are made to maintain focus and direction.

God never intended for us to step into life's battles without vision or direction. He calls us to prepare, to build spiritual endurance, and to square up with the enemy only after we've equipped ourselves with His truth. Our victory doesn't depend on the size of the opponent or the years of training behind us—it depends on who we fight with and how we fight.

Take Moses, for example. He started his "fight" before he was mentally or spiritually ready. Acting from impulse, he struck the Egyptian and fled into the wilderness. It took forty years before God called him back to face Pharaoh—this time, not in his own strength, but in divine partnership. Moses was out of sync with God's timing. When he separated himself in the desert, he finally heard not his own voice, but God's—preparing him for a greater impact on generations than he could have imagined. Sister, when we sit in our quiet places of prayer and stillness, we invite His will and voice into our lives to do great things for His glory, purpose, and plan.

Contrast that with Sylvester Stallone's journey as an artist. He didn't wait forty years like Moses, but it did take two decades for him to evolve through Rocky II, Rocky III, and Rocky IV. Each film revealed a different kind of fight—one that tested not just the body, but the spirit.

In life, your greatest battles will rarely be with other people—they're internal. They're about fear, distraction, procrastination, and unbelief. God's Word reminds us: "The weapons of our warfare are not carnal but mighty through God to the pulling down of strongholds" (2 Corinthians 10:4). That means the real training happens in prayer, study, surrender, and daily discipline.

So when you ask, "Why do I have to fight?"—remember, the fight refines you. It builds spiritual muscle. It transforms your mindset from survival to strategy. And it teaches you to depend on God's strength rather than your own.

You may not feel ready for the ring. But if you trust the process, prepare your mind, and put your faith to work, you'll discover that every punch you throw in faith lands with divine precision.

Chapter 2
The Devil Picks the Fight, but with God, We Win

Once you've squared up, don't be surprised when the enemy steps in.

I still remember the day someone stole my purse when I was twenty. Instinct took over, and before I knew it, I was in a physical fight. Thankfully, a security guard intervened before things went too far—and by God's grace, I wasn't arrested.

For a long time, I carried shame and regret about that moment. But over the years, God gave me a new perspective. That incident taught me about possession, power, and purpose—and how easily we can react before thinking. At the time, I was a young social worker, unaware of how one wrong decision could change everything. Like Moses, I acted out of emotion instead of wisdom.

Looking back, I realize the fight wasn't really about the purse. It was about a perceived threat to my dignity, my future, and what mattered most to me. That's exactly how the enemy works. The devil doesn't fight you over small things; he targets your future and your promises with God. He stirs up distractions, conflict, and doubt to make you forget what you're called to do.

The Fight for the Promiseland

Scripture reminds us, "We are not ignorant of his devices" (2 Corinthians 2:11). Sometimes those "devices" appear as thoughts that whisper defeat; other times, they're circumstances that provoke frustration or fear.

When I think about this book—*Battle Strategies for Victorious Women*—I see it as a roadmap for those moments when the devil picks a fight with your purpose. Women are called to be creators, change agents, and living testimonies of God's glory. That's why the enemy attacks our promises, our passions, and our sense of worth.

There are many reasons women hesitate to fight. Society has often told us, "Good girls don't fight," or, "Just accept whatever happens." But God is raising a generation of women who know that fighting—in faith—is not rebellion. It's obedience. It's the decision to protect what God has entrusted to you: your peace, your family, your dream, your destiny.

Eleanor Roosevelt once said, "No one can make you feel inferior without your consent." We are not inferior—we are equipped. God has given us power and authority to stand firm. It's time to shift our mindset from passive acceptance to active partnership with Heaven.

Squaring Off with the Enemy

To square off means to take a decisive position—to face your opponent head-on with strategy and resolve. In every battle, there is a victor and a challenger, and what determines the outcome is preparation.

When Scripture says, "The battle belongs to the Lord," it doesn't mean we do nothing. It means we engage in obedience while God handles the outcome. Our role is readiness—mental, spiritual, and practical. The Lord said, "From the days of John the Baptist until now the kingdom of heaven suffereth violence, and the violent take it by force" (Matthew 11:12, KJV).

Fighting in faith involves more than emotion. It requires values, tactics, and constant reassessment. You must know what's at stake, who stands with you, and what tools you'll use. You don't enter battle without armor—and our armor is prayer, truth, righteousness, and peace (Ephesians 6:10–17).

The fight isn't meant to defeat you; it's meant to develop you. God trains your hands for war and your fingers for battle (Psalm 144:1). Through every challenge, He strengthens your resolve and reveals His strategy.

Chapter 3
Decisions

Making decisions has always been a challenge for me. Some choices I can resolve quickly—right or wrong, yes or no. But others tug at the heart. When people, purpose, or emotion are involved, clarity doesn't always come easily. Over the years, though, I've learned that the gray areas shrink when we allow God to illuminate them. The unknown becomes less frightening when we trust that He is already in our future.

There was a time when indecision felt safer than movement. I'd hesitate, analyze, and delay. But the truth is, not deciding is still a decision—one that often costs us time, peace, and opportunity. The residue of indecision leaves imbalance and regret. I've learned that delayed obedience can sometimes mean delayed blessing.

I imagine the children of Israel faced similar fears when they were offered freedom after generations of slavery. Stepping into the unknown looked terrifying. Remaining in the familiar—though painful—felt safer. Yet a few among them dared to dream of something better, not only for themselves but for their children and grandchildren. It only took a handful of people willing to hope, pray, and believe for God to move.

God has always been the Master Decision-Maker. He knew the end from the beginning; He designed your path before you ever walked it. His decisions were already prepared for the challenges you would face. "For I know the plans I have for you," declares the Lord, "plans to prosper you and not to harm you, plans to give you a future and a hope" (Jeremiah 29:11).

So if His grace is sufficient, why do we still struggle to move forward? Often, it's because we mistake options for decisions.

Options vs. Decisions

Let's pause for a moment and define the difference.

• **A decision** is a decisive act—a commitment to move forward in a chosen direction.

• **An option** is an evaluation of possibilities before the decision is made.

Here's an example:

"I've decided to go back to school."

That's a decision—a firm commitment.

"I can choose between online or hybrid classes."

Those are options—different ways to fulfill the decision.

The two are related, but they serve different purposes. Decisions move us. Options inform us.

Sometimes we confuse the two, especially in matters of the heart—relationships, jobs, ministries, or life changes. We linger between choices, counting the cost but fearing the consequence. Yet indecision keeps us planted in soil that no longer feeds our growth.

Like a plant that has outgrown its flowerpot, staying too long in the same environment can stunt our roots. The pot that once nourished us can start to limit us.

If you've ever moved a plant, you know how it reacts—the roots resist, the soil shifts, and the plant droops for a while. But after a time, with fresh space and light, it grows stronger. Change works the same way. Growth is uncomfortable, but necessary.

Ask yourself:

Lord, what lessons do You want me to learn as I grow and change?

How can I use these lessons to move closer to Your promise and plans?

Stay or Leave

Every major life season brings us to this question: Do I stay, or do I leave?

The children of Israel had to face this. They could remain in Egypt, in bondage and familiarity, or trust Moses and follow God into the unknown. Freedom required a decision. Hope required a risk.

I've faced this crossroads, too. When I decided to go back to school, I had several options—promotion at work, a new job, or continuing on the same path. But the decision to return to school was about ownership of my future. It meant no longer letting others define my direction. It was difficult, but liberating.

From that experience, I learned three truths about making God-led decisions:

1 Trust God in the process. His process is rarely linear. You can count the cost, but you'll never see every turn. "His ways are higher than our ways."

2 Believe in something bigger. Even when the path is unclear,

God's promises remain. "All things work together for good to them that love God" (Romans 8:28).

3 Have faith through the unknowns. Faith isn't the absence of fear—it's the decision to move forward anyway, knowing who walks with you.

When Options Expire

Sometimes what once worked no longer fits. An old habit, a familiar role, a comfortable situation—it used to serve you, but now it feels restrictive. God allows this discomfort to signal it's time to grow.

Remaining in a place you've outgrown can feel like riding a roller coaster that never stops—round and round, no end in sight. Yet knowing who rides with you makes all the difference. When Jesus is in your seat, the twists and turns don't feel quite as frightening.

Joshua faced a similar moment. Stepping into Moses' role couldn't have been easy, but God reassured him: "Every place where you set your foot will be yours" (Joshua 1:3). The same promise holds true for you. As you step into new territory, God steps with you.

Chapter 4
Difficult but Necessary

There it was again—the pile of clean clothes that nobody had put away. I walked past it for the third time, pretending not to see it, but the pile stared back at me like a quiet accusation. "It's not my turn," I told myself. "It's not fair."

The truth was, I was tired of doing everything—tired of feeling like someone else always owed me help. Those clothes weren't just clothes; they were a symbol of my frustration and the imbalance I felt.

As I stood there, I closed my eyes and imagined a "special laundry angel" folding everything, spraying each piece with heavenly fragrance. I smiled at the thought, half in humor, half in wishful thinking. But when I opened my eyes, the clothes were still there—waiting. And I realized: this is my responsibility. The same hands that washed them must be the hands that fold them.

That moment felt small but sacred. God used it to whisper: Sometimes the things that annoy you are the very things I'm using to train you.

Bold Step of Change

The Fight for the Promiseland

When David fought Goliath, it was an ordinary day—until it wasn't. David didn't wake up planning to be a hero; he simply went to deliver food to his brothers. But something shifted when he heard the Philistine mocking God. Righteous anger rose within him. He couldn't ignore the disrespect toward his Father. That's when David partnered with God—and that partnership defined his life.

Sometimes, change begins when we get fed up—when we realize something must shift because staying still dishonors what God has placed inside us. Maybe it's poverty, a toxic relationship, a stalled career, or self-doubt. Something inside us finally says, "No more. My story will not end here."

We all reach moments that demand bold change. It might start with something small—the same way that buzzing fly in your house eventually drives you to act.

Last summer, I remember relaxing after work, listening to smooth jazz, when I heard it—the faint hum of a fly. I tried to ignore it, but it kept buzzing, louder and louder. Finally, I said aloud, "This ends tonight!" I grabbed a fly swatter and took action. It sounds silly, but I believe God gives us that same kind of inner urgency about our promised lands. When something keeps buzzing in your spirit— nudging you, agitating you—it's usually the Holy Spirit saying, "Do something."

We often miss God's rhythm because we resist His momentum. But if we pause long enough to listen, that irritation becomes invitation— an opportunity to partner with Him for progress.

What Are You Willing to Stand Up For?

What's worth fighting for in your life right now?

What threatens your future that you know must be settled?

What keeps buzzing in your heart that God is asking you to finally face?

These are holy questions—because every decision to act requires courage, and every act of courage moves you closer to the promise.

When we look at other dreamers and promise-seekers in Scripture—Abraham, Esther, Ruth, Nehemiah—they all reached a moment where obedience was uncomfortable but necessary. Their "yes" cost them something—but it also positioned them for purpose.

So take courage. The next step may feel difficult, but it's necessary. And God is in it with you.

Chapter 5
Clarity

Clarity with God

God calls each of us to be clear about our relationship with Him—what we want, what we need, and what truly matters. His Word is already clear about His intentions toward us: "For all the promises of God in Him are Yes, and in Him Amen, to the glory of God" (2 Corinthians 1:20).

If His plans for us are good, then our part is to approach Him with open hearts and honest motives. Clarity begins with alignment—our thoughts, attitudes, and behaviors agreeing with His truth. When our internal world is cluttered, it's hard to receive divine direction.

The Israelites understood deliverance but not destiny. They were clear about leaving Egypt, but not about where they were going. God, however, was crystal clear: He wanted relationship, not just relocation. The same is true for us—He desires communion, not confusion.

Clarity keeps life in order. When we lose sight of why we're doing something, we also lose our way. Jesus said, "You shall know the truth, and the truth shall make you free" (John 8:32). Freedom requires focus. Confusion invites the enemy.

In-Between Places

We all walk through seasons that no longer satisfy the soul—those "in-between" places. The job that once excited us now drains us. The home we once loved suddenly feels small. The squeaky door that used to make us laugh becomes a daily irritation.

I once ignored a loose board on my porch for months. After tripping over it twice, I finally realized: the risk of not fixing it was greater than the inconvenience of change.

That's how God works. He lets discomfort remind us that stagnation is unsafe. Clarity often begins with agitation.

So when something keeps "buzzing" in your environment—like that fly that refuses to leave your living room—it may be God's nudge to act. Peace isn't the absence of noise; it's the decision to address what steals your focus.

Seeing, Saying, and Thinking

• What are you seeing?

The Israelites said, "We were in our own sight as grasshoppers" (Numbers 13:33).

Clarity requires honest vision—seeing yourself and your situation as God sees them. Are you focusing on beginnings, middles, or endings? On light or shadow? Faith is the lens that adjusts the focus.

• What are you saying?

"The power of life and death is in the tongue" (Proverbs 18:21).

Words either clarify or cloud. When God shapes our speech, He accelerates abundance. As we declare faith, the noise of unbelief grows quieter. Try saying aloud each morning: "If God be for me, who can be against me?" (Romans 8:31).

• **What are you thinking?**

Clarity also dwells in the mind. Have you ever dreamed so vividly that you could taste the air or feel the breeze—and woke up believing it was possible? That glimpse of hope is God's preview of potential. Guard your thoughts; they are the soil where clarity grows. "Let this mind be in you, which was also in Christ Jesus" (Philippians 2:5).

The Rhythm of Change

Something better must first happen inside us before it shows around us. "Better" speaks of determination, perseverance, and patience. God promises, "I will pour out a blessing so great that there will not be room enough to receive it" (Malachi 3:10).

Overflow implies movement—one vessel pouring into another. When we cooperate with that flow, we experience renewal.

The Israelites had to redefine what "better" meant. Their new land didn't look like their imagination, but it was still God's provision. Likewise, clarity teaches us to trust God in the middle, not only at the start or the finish. The same God who led them out also led them through.

Something better is always possible when we open our eyes to growth, possibility, and the guidance of the Holy Spirit. That inner stirring—the sense that "there must be more"—is not restlessness; it's revelation.

So pause and ask:

Lord, what does my "better" look like? For my family? My community? My future?

How are You speaking clarity and confirmation to me through my thoughts, dreams, and visions?

Chapter 6
Walking to the Other Side

When I first started walking a few years ago, I didn't feel ready. My doctor and I agreed it was time to focus on health and wellness, but enthusiasm was the last thing I felt. My feet hurt for months—even with the right shoes and a plan. Every step reminded me how long it had been since I'd really moved. Still, I kept walking.

At first, "the other side" simply meant halfway down the mall or to the end of the track. But I learned something: "the other side" changes as you do. What once seemed far becomes familiar. Each new step builds strength, endurance, and confidence.

We all have our own "walks." For some, it's health; for others, forgiveness, faith, or freedom. Whatever your path, God meets you in the movement. The children of Israel had to take their first steps into an unknown wilderness. Their journey required faith in a promise they couldn't yet see. They trusted Moses' vision until it became their own.

Hope is what keeps us walking. It's the expectation that if we keep moving—if we put in the time, energy, and trust—something will change for the better. President Barack Obama called it "the audacity of hope." It's the boldness to believe that what lies ahead will outshine what's behind.

Even now, as I write these words, the world faces conflicts and uncertainties—reminders that hope is not passive; it's a strategy of faith. Hope keeps us moving forward when fear says stand still.

So, keep walking. Walk through the pain, the disappointment, the in-between. God doesn't just wait for you on the other side—He walks with you through every mile.

Something Better

Of all the themes in this book, "something better" may be the hardest to define—because it looks different for each of us. For one, it might be a new career; for another, emotional healing; for another still, a deeper faith. But every "better" begins as a thought—a small whisper that says, "This isn't all there is."

That yearning for something better is sacred. It's the Holy Spirit awakening vision inside you. It calls you upward—to a higher purpose, a greater peace, a fuller life.

"Forgetting those things which are behind, and reaching forth unto those things which are before, I press toward the mark for the prize of the high calling of God in Christ Jesus" (Philippians 3:13–14).

Better is not vanity—it's vision. It's that melody in your heart that won't stop playing. It's the same divine song that inspires you to break generational cycles, create legacies of faith, and believe that grace and growth can coexist.

Grace and faith work together like rhythm and melody. Grace gives you the space to try; faith gives you the courage to act. In the stillness —when ideas are born and dreams are whispered—God reveals the greatness He sees in you: the strong woman, the beloved daughter, the creator made in His image.

Your value isn't defined by what others see or say. You are defined by the One who calls you "chosen." Forget what lies behind—old doubts, missed chances, familiar fears—and press toward the "better" God prepared for you.

"For God has not given us a spirit of fear, but of power, and of love, and of a sound mind" (2 Timothy 1:7). That power is the strength to change; that love is the courage to try again; that sound mind is the clarity to know when to move forward.

Walking to the other side means walking with God, step by step, even when others don't understand your path. The children of Israel struggled with the same tension—longing for freedom but missing familiarity. They forgot that the unfamiliar was where God's miracles happened.

We, too, wrestle with double-mindedness—wanting better, yet clinging to what's comfortable. But better always demands change. If we can't change the circumstance, we can let God change our mindset.

That's what walking does—it transforms the way we think about distance, pain, and progress. Each step forward proves that even when it hurts, you're healing. Even when it's slow, you're growing.

Keep walking.

Keep hoping.

Keep believing there's something better—because there is.

And remember: even if your steps are small, they still count. God measures faith, not distance.

Chapter 7
My Future Awaits Me

The Strategy of Selection

I'm an avid reader and a lifelong sports fan. Every spring, I tune in to watch the NFL Draft. It fascinates me—not just the excitement of who gets chosen, but the strategy behind each decision. Teams study players' strengths, character, and chemistry. They ask: Does this person fit our vision? Our offense? Our defense? Our future?

Each draft pick is a blend of promise and purpose. Teams don't just recruit talent; they recruit alignment.

That's exactly how God works with us. He is the ultimate Master Strategist—placing each of us on the right team, in the right position, at the right time. He knows who we are, what we bring, and where we'll thrive. We may not always understand His draft choices—why certain people or seasons come and go—but His plan is perfect.

"For we are His workmanship, created in Christ Jesus for good works, which God prepared beforehand that we should walk in them" (Ephesians 2:10).

The Fight for the Promiseland

Your role, your calling, your gifts—they're not random. You were chosen on purpose for a purpose. God doesn't make trades or bench players. He equips and deploys them. He knew you before the foundation of the earth—whom He knew, He predestined and chose. Thank you, God, for choosing me.

The Race of Faith

I also love the show *The Amazing Race*. Every season, contestants line up—excited, nervous, ready to run. They don't know where the journey will take them, but they believe it will be worth it. There's something thrilling about that kind of faith.

Life is much the same. We start the race of destiny not knowing every turn, but trusting the One who mapped it out. The future awaits all of us—but not everyone believes it's for them.

The Israelites, after 400 years in Egypt, had to relearn what it meant to hope again. When Moses said, "Get up and walk," some hesitated. Freedom sounded beautiful, but it also sounded dangerous. They believed deliverance was possible for someone else, not themselves. Yet God had already prepared their future—a land flowing with milk and honey.

Many of them never saw it, not because it wasn't promised, but because they doubted they belonged there. "We were in our own sight as grasshoppers," they said (Numbers 13:33).

Faith requires the courage to see beyond giants—to believe that your future is meant for you. Only two spies, Joshua and Caleb, saw what God saw: a future worth fighting for. They knew that struggle and destiny often walk hand in hand.

Your race will test you too. But remember—the same God who invited you to run is the One waiting at the finish line.

"Let us run with patience the race that is set before us, looking unto Jesus, the author and finisher of our faith" (Hebrews 12:1–2).

The Promise of the Future

Your future isn't some faraway dream—it's unfolding right now. God's plan for you is exceedingly, abundantly above all that you can ask or imagine (Ephesians 3:20). So think positively about where you're going. Expect goodness, not scarcity; progress, not paralysis.

The children of Israel struggled because the unfamiliar frightened them. But the unfamiliar is often where God performs His greatest miracles. Don't despise small beginnings or uncomfortable transitions —they're proof that growth is happening.

God sees not your broken pieces but your wholeness in Him. He sees holiness, resilience, and beauty. "When God saw it, He said it was good." And if He called it good, it still is. You are the apple of His eye. You are fearfully and wonderfully made.

Something better is not a distant hope—it's a living promise. It starts with faith and matures through obedience. Your value isn't based on others' opinions or definitions of success. You were handcrafted by the Creator, and His plan for you includes joy, peace, wisdom, and abundance.

"For God has not given us a spirit of fear, but of power, love, and a sound mind" (2 Timothy 1:7).

So hold your head high. Keep running your race. Keep trusting the process. The Promised Land isn't behind you—it's just ahead.

Your future awaits. And God is already there.

About the Author

The author is...